Locums Lifestyle

Take Control of Your Life and Make Great Money

By: Lorraine Barron, MD

Locums Lifestyle
1923 Bragg St #140-2543
Sanford, NC 27330
www.LocumsLifestyle.org

Copyright © 2013 by Lorraine Barron, MD

All rights reserved. No part of this book may be copied, transmitted or stored in a database without permission.

DISCLAIMER

This book is not intended as medical advice. It is also not intended to prevent, diagnose, treat or cure disease. Instead the book is intended only to share the unofficial research and opinion of the author. The information is provided for educational purposes only, not as treatment instructions for any disease or ailment. Much of the book is a statement of opinion in areas where the facts are controversial or do not exist. The information in this book should not be considered any more valid than any other type of informal opinion.

The information was not written to replace the advice or care of a qualified health care professional. Be sure to check with your own qualified health care provider before beginning any protocols or procedures discussed in this book, or before stopping or altering any diet, lifestyle, or other therapies previously recommended to you by your health care provider.

The treatments described in this book may have side effects and carry other known and unknown risks and health hazards. The statements in this book have not been evaluated by the United States FDA. Use of the information in this book is at your own risk.

This book is dedicated to Carl and Olivia.
Who remind me daily that I can't take money or work with me when I die.

A Message to All Locum Tenens

Are you tired of not having control of your career, your time and your money? Have you changed jobs hoping things would "get better", only to find it's "the same stuff" just a different location? Do you need additional income that your current job doesn't provide, but don't want to quit yet? Do you feel like your "job" is to just continue and take the abuse no matter the risk to your patients or your malpractice record? Do you want to try other jobs (including non-clinical ones), but don't have the time or flexibility to explore your options? Are you uncertain about your job security with the ACA (aka *ObamaScare*) changes ahead?

My name is Dr. Lorraine Barron, like you, I've been in those situations and I want to share with you what I have learned and what the Locums Lifestyle can provide.

Being a full time Locum Tenens has allowed me to maintain control of my non-clinical life, schedule, income and working environment that an office based or employed position can no longer provide. Like many physicians, I was under the "old" mindset that I needed to be "employed" with all the benefits in order to feel secure —not true!

To this date, I have used Locum Tenens in my career for about every possible reason and opportunity —to making fast and easy money, exploring other jobs and positions, to even taking some time off and freeing my schedule for my family (just because I felt like it) and most of all, reducing my work schedule without reducing my income.

In sharing with you what I have learned from my experience as a Locum Tenens, It is my sincere goal to help physicians gain control of their careers and realize their possibilities. For those of you who want to experience the career and lifestyle I'm living www.LocumsLifestyle.org/sign-up now and take control of your future. For more inquiries on the Locums Lifestyle, feel free to send me an email.

All the best,

Lorraine Barron, MD

drbarron@locumslifestyle.org

TABLE OF CONTENTS

Getting Started as Locums 7
Chapter 1- Deciding on Your Business Structure 10
    Arranging Separate Credit Cards and Bank Accounts 11
    Taxes 12
    Using Your Spouse as an Employee 12
    How You Get Paid 13
    Expenses 14
Chapter 2- Networking 17
    Searching For a Job as a Locum Tenens 17
    Where to Find Jobs 19
    Using Google Voice 20
    Credentialing 21
    Malpractice 22
    How to Quit your "Day Job" as an Employed Physician 24
Chapter 3- Preparation for Jobs 27
    Packing 27
    Duplicate Items 28
    Hospital Paperwork 29
    Fast Food 30
    Choosing a Hotel 31
    Renting a Car 34
    RVs 36
Chapter 4- Starting a New Job 38
    Your First Day 38
    Orientation 41
    Time Tracking 43
    Uniforms 44
    Networking 45
Recommended Reading 46
About The Author 51

Introduction

Like many physicians, I finished Residency with the expectation that I would find a good position and stay there for the rest of my career. Like many other physicians, I found out that it doesn't always work that way. The first group I joined post residency was collegial, smart, hard working and fair. That was the last group I worked for that would have all of those traits at the same time. But, as my 7 on/7 off schedule worked its way into my first 18 months, I realized that my schedule was compressed and most of my "7 off" was spent catching up. I wanted to go on vacation with my family without killing myself. I was forced to work double before or after the trip and having to wheel-n-deal with partners for it. I realized that it was no longer physically or mentally possible for me to keep on the treadmill. That was the beginning of learning: **The 4 Lessons of Locums.**

Getting Started as Locums

I decided to "take control" of my career and schedule, and open up a small, low overhead practice closer to family. Please continue with the story when you stop laughing at the first stupid "career" move I made —as dumb as it was— it gave me my first taste of the "locums" life. It was the main source of my income and it was promptly eaten by my practice. It did, however, keep me from going bankrupt.

That was **Lesson #1: Locums makes you MONEY... FAST!** Whether it's paying off student loans, office debts, or your mortgage, it's a fast way to deal with a temporary problem. Once I realized that the health insurance companies were going to pay me less the Medicare rates, and my overhead was to the point where my practice was going to just continue to be an "expensive hobby", I then stumbled upon the second use of being a Locum.

Lesson #2: Locums lets you explore other jobs and network to find other positions. Like many physicians, I was under the "old" mindset that I needed to be "employed" with all the benefits in order to feel "secure". Through networking with other "hopeful docs", I tried 3 other "employed" positions with each opportunity taking shorter and shorter times to "figure" out that all of the programs ran on 18-24 month cycles of boom and bust. These included some with positions as "director". Once again thinking, "If I had more influence, I could fix the situation". Yes, you can stop laughing at that one, too. That was probably my biggest realization —as long as you are employed, you lack control of your work.

It also taught me **Lesson #3: As Locums, you are paid for what you work**. Being employed, I figured out that an administrator could increase my workload without increasing my pay, force me to work overtime and, too many times, my "bonus" was lost to incompetent billers when it was RVU (relative value unit) based. At the urging of a friend doing full time Locums, I decided to drop my "employed" mindset and became a Freelance physician.

When I started my first couple of jobs as a fulltime freelancer, I quickly realized that I was FINALLY in control of what working conditions, what schedule, and how much pay I'm willing to accept. I then realized, **Lesson #4: Locums let YOU decide what working conditions you're willing to accept and for what price**. I took lower paying jobs that had an "easy schedule" and I jacked up the rate ($200+/hr.) for busy, poorly structured, short notice or holiday work. I can negotiate the hotel, car, schedule and even the number of encounters. As these different groups go through the "boom and bust" cycles, I adjust my rate and schedule based on what I WANT to work with. If the workload gets out of control or abusive, I just either lower my exposure or "take a break" until they figure it out and improve conditions. It's not personal, *it's all business*. Now, I get PTSD every time someone suggests I take an employed position!

Introduction

The goal of this book is to give other physicians a guide to either add income to their current position or take the path many others are taking to a great Locums Lifestyle. I hope this guide can give you the career and lifestyle it's given me.

Chapter 1 - Deciding on Your Business Structure

When you decide to go freelance and set up your own Locum Tenens business, the most important decision you have to make is the structure of your business. Do you want to set up a Limited Liability Company (LLC) or form a Standard corporation (S-Corp)? Perhaps you would prefer to be the sole proprietor. This is not a decision to be taken lightly and everything should be discussed in detail with your accountant. This is essential before you make any decision that will affect the future of your business. If you are dealing with a general practice lawyer, they may not fully understand the financial implications so make sure you engage a tax lawyer. Consider visiting your accountant first so you have all the financial figures in front of you when you see your lawyer. You need to take legal advice before forming the business, not only for ratification purposes but the choice of structure will also protect your separate business from personal assets. It does not, however, protect you from malpractice.

The main difference between being a Sole Proprietor and being an LLC/ S-Corp is the Federal Employment Identification Number. This number will be helpful when you are dealing with tax returns as it enables you to leave your social security number off on most of your invoices. There are no other notable variations between being an LLC and being a sole proprietor as both structures separate your "business" from your personal assets if ever an issue with contracting should arise. Forming a Standard Corporation is more complicated and more costly as it involves paying yourself a wage from the company if you are taking taxes out. You will also need to hire a payroll company to issue your own paycheck. It is up to you to decide how much money you are going to take out of the business and when you want your paycheck paid, weekly or monthly.

Most Locum Tenens opt for an LLC because of the added complications connected to a standard corporation, but your accountant should advise you on the best possible option. The structure of any freelance business is very important and you need to get it right from the start. You have to keep personal finances separate from your business income and expenditures; otherwise, you will find sorting out your tax returns very time-consuming.

ARRANGING SEPARATE CREDIT CARDS AND BANK ACCOUNTS

It is very important to get a separate credit card for your business and a good one to use is the American Express Business Card because it will allow you to put all your business expenses on one card without giving you a pre-set spending limit. This will be useful if you are in another state or country and you need to purchase an emergency plane ticket to get home, or if you have any unexpected expenditures you haven't taken into account. With an unlimited expenditure credit card you will be able to do this without any problems. If you have a pre-set limit, you may find yourself in an emergency wherein you are very near or over that limit and you cannot make the purchase or pay for the travel ticket you need. By having a separate business card you will easily be able to keep track of your monthly expenditures as everything will be listed on the monthly statements and they will not get mixed up with your personal spending.

You should also set up a business bank account with an online banking facility so you can monitor your account when you are away from home. It is very important for you to have access to your account even when you are traveling. Opt for a good bank such as Wells Fargo or the Bank of America. At the same time, look for one that does not charge fees for every business transaction. When your accounts are inspected each year, your auditor will need to see your bank account and will not want to plough through personal items. It also makes your tax returns much easier to fill up and you can see how your business is doing financially.

When you are working on your tax returns, several of your expenses can be offset against tax so you will be able to increase your monthly income quite quickly. Examples of these are your cell phone, fax machine, legal fees and other things connected with your business that are also tax deductible. Your accountant will be able to tell you what these are and even his fees are tax deductible. You may very well be surprised to find which things can be used to offset to your tax bill.

TAXES

Once you decide to run your own business, you will have absolute control of your money and you also get to decide how much to take out of the business itself. When you were an employee and received a set amount of wage, you are now in charge. When you were employed, your take home pay was "set". You probably had to work on a tight budget and were unable to splash out on a luxury item if you felt like it. Getting to splurge is one of the perks you can indulge in once in a while when you run a successful business that is making money. Locums are always in demand and you can set your own rates for the job depending on where you are working month to month or year to year —your decision.

USING YOUR SPOUSE AS AN EMPLOYEE

There are a number of independent companies where husband-and-wife teams run the company together but only one of them is officially paid a wage for tax reasons. If one is working as an Administrative assistant and drawing up schedules, making appointments and phone calls, not only is their job tax deductible, they can also receive a paycheck from your company. This means you can provide a 401k and other benefits too.

How You Get Paid

Once you have decided on your preferred business structure and the business has been set up, it is up to you how much you pay yourself. And, if you decide to pay yourself $150 per hour, which is the rate for working in a busy hospital, that will be your take-home pay without any deductions. Whenever you receive money in your business account (usually direct deposit), you need to keep track of the totals across different states to fill up your tax return to the IRS. You should receive a 1099 from the locums company prior to the tax filing dates the same time you would have received a W-2. You will not receive a W-2 unless you have an S-Corp and then it will be directly from your corporation. Your S-Corp can be set up in such a way that you pay yourself a "set amount" of wage on a monthly or biweekly basis along with "bonuses". When you have an idea of how much you plan on working, this is easier. If you ever decide to change your work schedule from a monthly basis, it can be more difficult to manage with an S-corp.

If you are a freelance working for a locum company, they will usually pay for any car rentals, hotels and airline tickets if needed without the expenses being taken off from your business account or you having to submit invoices. Gas is usually reimbursed after submitting the receipt.

The locums company does not cover meals but they are deductible so keep track of them. Most people rent a car for work rather than using their own cars because they will only get paid the current rate per mile. In this sense, you can also lease a car under your business and the locums company will pay you by the mile and those that aren't covered will be deductible on your taxes. Talk with your accountant prior to setting it up because there are usage restrictions and other tax implications.

You will need to fill up a self-employment tax form then you can decide whether you wish to pay the tax monthly, quarterly, or annually, and no tax will be deducted from your paycheck. Be careful not to delay too much in paying your taxes. There can be filing penalties and getting a "surprise" tax bill at the end of the year is never fun.

How much will you make? It's up to you! The best thing about running your own business is the flexibility it gives you. You can work 5-7 days a month instead of working full time and you can take a time off when you want to. Some people working for fill-in-doctor jobs work three days a week or a month to pay for their kids' college fees, other locums are doing it to pay off student loans. If you wish to go traveling in Europe for a couple of months, you wouldn't need to ask permission from anyone else but yourself. Some locum doctors work for 3 months and take time off for another 3. While others just take the summers off, there are those who prefer to take the "busy" winters off. In any case, your work schedule is whatever you decide it to be.

EXPENSES

The biggest advantage of doing freelance work is the expenditure you can offset against tax but you have to be very organized to run your own business. Papers and invoices have to be filed away and you must keep accounts for everything as they need to be audited once a year. The more things that are tax deductible, the less you will pay in taxes, but you need to keep every single receipt. If you are traveling, it is a good idea to take a folder with you with an envelope in it to put your receipts in as you get them. If you have chosen the American Express card, all your expenses will appear on their monthly

Chapter 1- Deciding on Your Business Structure

statements and these should be kept in date order. You will not have to go through every single receipt but you do need to keep them as they will have to be submitted to the IRS if they wish to see them. And your accountant will need to look at them if they are helping you with your tax return. We will discuss on how to make tracking easier later in the series.

If you are self-employed, you also need to take out health insurance as it will no longer be taken out of your wages. If your wife is working for the company and you employ anyone else, you can put in for group health insurance. Of course, there are major changes in the insurance industry this year. You will most likely end up on the Health Insurance Exchange (HIE). However, at this point it is impossible to give recommendations as even the insurance companies lack the information to define the coverage of the HIE plans or the cost. Stay tuned to the website as we will be updating the information as it comes.

Automobile expenses are also tax deductible, as well as meals and other food when you are traveling. If you are meeting a patient or client for a business meal, it is also 50% tax deductible providing you keep the receipt.

You need to make sure you have a reliable cell phone, consider a virtual mailbox, iPad/ laptop computer and a good email server. If your spouse works for the company and needs to call you regularly to check schedules and appointments, you can also purchase a small cell phone for them out of company funds if it will be used regularly and that is also tax deductible too.

Because you will be dealing with a lot of people you do not know and they will be checking your credentials such as your date of birth and social security number, it is advisable to invest in a credit locking service like Equifax as this will prevent identification theft. It stays "locked" until you release it for a purchase or credit check and they will also notify you if there are any changes to your credit. You do not have to be a locum to have your identity and credit stolen. Anyone who comes into contact with strangers is a viable target. Doctors are recommended to invest in a credit locking service as well because identity fraud is on the increase.

If you have set up an office in your own home and you are claiming tax relief on it, you will need to discuss this fully with your accountant. All the equipment in the room, including the office equipment, stationery, Internet service, telephone, and fax machine can be offset against tax. However, you need to make sure this room is used only as an office for your business and you do not have any surplus items of furniture in the room. You cannot have a spare bed, chest of drawers, or a wardrobe in there. For instance, if you have turned a spare bedroom into your office, these items must be removed as soon as your business is up and running.

If you do not intend to offset this home office against tax, then you can have other items in there but if you are claiming for an office, it has to be solely used as an office or you could be in trouble from the tax department.

Setting your business structure correctly will save you a lot of stress and time later, along with setting up the "mindset" that your labor is your money and your business.

Chapter 2 - Networking

If you are a qualified doctor who enjoys the variety and freedom of working as a locum tenens, how do you go about finding available jobs that fit your needs? More and more doctors are switching to locum jobs now as they are tired of the uncompensated overtime and lack of control they receive working as a permanent member of the hospital staff.

Here are some helpful hints on how to find a locum job and set you on the road to being a successful independent contractor.

Searching For a Job as a Locum Tenens

The best way to find fill-in doctor jobs is to learn how to network and keep on networking and networking. Locums love talking about their experiences in various hospitals they have worked in or are currently working under. And unlike other business vacancies, there are often more jobs available than there are locums to fill them.

Some statistics say there are 14 jobs to every doctor who wants to work as a locum tenens. That is because fewer and fewer doctors want to work full time in hospitals for long hours and low pay. They prefer the freedom of choice that working as a locum gives them and the variety of jobs available. Hospitals and locum companies are desperate to find locums to fill the vacancies even if locum tenens are more expensive to employ. Very few locums are worried about competition and they like to help each other by swapping views of their experiences and passing on contact details and connections to other locum tenens.

Experienced locums know the best and the worst places to work and will be happy to pass on contact details for vacant positions. Networking will also enable you to learn the current rates of pay and prevent you from selling yourself short. Some contracts prevent locums from revealing their actual salary but they are all happy to say they would not work for less than a certain amount of dollars per hour.

This is particularly useful to newcomers to the locum tenens circuit who probably are unaware of what rate they should be asking for based on the conditions of a particular job situation. By learning the minimum rate their colleagues are asking, they will soon realize they have priced themselves too low and will be able to ask for a higher rate when the next job comes up.

If a locum tenens informs new recruits that they will not work for less than $140 an hour, and they will get paid $110 an hour, perhaps by the same company or hospital, they know they were ripped off and will negotiate a higher rate for the next job. That is why networking is vitally important for anyone looking for a locum tenens job.

Because locums move from job to job, they all want to pick each other's brain about the best places to work. If they hear a hospital is very busy and they will be expected to work long hours, they will be able to negotiate for a higher rate. If you find out it's a "cushy" position, near home, and easy work, you might not want to negotiate so hard. Every locum has his or her own opinion and a colleague might not share it. Just because you hear a bad report of a hospital, it does not mean you should turn down a job there. Listen to what the locum has to say and be prepared for the pitfalls they spoke about. As long as the group, company or hospital does not jeopardize your license to practice, you can make up your own mind whether you want to work for them or not, how long you want to work, and what your acceptable rate might be.

Chapter 2- Networking

Locum Tenens are in such demand that they can decide how many days a week or month they want to work. If they only want to work 3 or 4 days a week or even 3 or 4 days a month, they can have this written into their contract. Some of the hospitals may advertise 7 days on/ 7 days off. However, they are not using a locum unless they have a significant need and most are eventually willing to negotiate even when not up front about it. If they don't, remember "it's business" and it's reasonable to move on to the next offer.

WHERE TO FIND JOBS

The best place to look for a job is on the Internet, just type in locum tenens into the subject bar and you will be surprised how many vacancies come up. Some websites list many different companies looking for locums and you will be delighted by the fact that there are so many job vacancies out there. There will be plenty of choices and you do not (and probably should not) have to take the first job you are offered.

Once you sign up with a locums company, they will be desperate to keep you in their books and they will constantly be calling you or sending you emails. If you do not want to answer the phone every time they call, you can use the Google program known as Google Voice which converts all missed calls into text messages. That way you can let your phone go to voicemail and then go through the text messages so you can choose any jobs that interest you before ringing the locum company back. You can make a note of the others and store them away for future use.

The best "company" to work with is one that finds you positions based on YOUR personal criteria. This is based on YOUR desired work conditions. For example: 10-shifts/month, no nights, no procedures and a great rate. Make it clear to the company that you will be working for whoever offers the best jobs at the best rates and say you may not stick to one particular company. That way you can increase the chances that they will "work for you" if they know they will be competing with other companies for your services. You may find yourself in a position where you are offered far better jobs than the ones you were originally looking for.

When you contact the person responsible for recruiting in the company, you need to mention right from the start what rates you are prepared to accept, what type of working conditions you want and what type of patients you want to see, for example children, the elderly or general. If you specialize in carrying out certain procedures, you should list that as well, as you will be able to ask for a higher rate with those additional skills. Ask the recruiter to email job vacancies through to you rather than phoning. It may not stop the calls but it should slow them down and give you more time to go through the jobs offered.

Prepare a good curriculum vitae (CV) with a clear timeline, but ask the company not to send it out to anyone until you are sure you want to work there. Once the company has sent your CV to a hospital, you are committed to work for that locums company and you are not allowed to work for any other company at THAT hospital/ group for the next two years.

USING GOOGLE VOICE

Google Voice is a program that converts your voicemails into text messages and saves them into audio. It then emails the audio to you so you can screen your calls. This service is free and you can always get a good idea who has called and the reason for their call, even if the translation of the voicemail gets a bit muddled. Google Voice also texts you the telephone number so you can just click on it and the phone will call it for you. All in all, it's very easy to use.

Chapter 2- Networking

It means you only have to talk to the people you want to talk to, and make sure you have a separate email account for your locum work. You can use Google Voice with Gmail as well as Yahoo. If you have a smart phone, add your locum email address to that as well.

When you speak to the recruiters about the job, at first they may not tell you much about it nor even give you the name of the hospital, but if it is fairly local and you have been networking, you will probably work out which hospital it is just from the description. For instance, they might tell you that the job is at a 450-bed hospital with two locum groups. You may already know the hospital or may have even worked there. Also, ask up front if it's one of the hospitals you're not willing to work with before they waste your time.

Always insist they email you a full description of the job so you will have written proof if you turn up and find it is not what you expected. Recruiters are not doctors nor members of the medical profession so they do not understand what makes malpractice a risk. Neither do they understand the word overworked as they make their money from the hours you work.

They would much prefer for you to work 7 days a week or 20 nights a month. When you get paid more, they get paid more. They will make more money from you working longer hours as opposed to you working a 3 or 4 days per week or month shift. The company may be all sweet and kind on the phone to you but they may not necessarily have your best interests at heart. I always recommend using the Job Screener which can be found on our website at www.LocumsLifestyle.org/job-screener, prior to officially accepting the position or negotiating the final work schedule and rate.

CREDENTIALING

This is the worst part of the job, but there are a few ways to make it less painful. The first thing the locum company does is to give your credentials and have you fill out their application form listing the date you graduated from medical school, your malpractice history and any other information the company needs to give you merit. They then use this information on the application forms for the hospitals, so every detail has to be filled out precisely and accurately.

If they do not ask for this information, you need to look for another locum company because they should be filling out the majority of your hospital applications with this information. It's a waste of time to fill out a new application every time you get a new position. However, be sure to "fact check" them, once it's filled out, you're still ultimately responsible for the content.

Scan all your certificates into your computer along with your DEA, your medical license, driver's license, vaccination records, your diplomas and any expiration dates in the title so you can keep track of everything. Make a credentials folder and put everything in there so you can just forward the folder every time you do credentialing.

Sometimes the size of the document causes a problem, so set it in black and white with low pixel so it will be carried on when you save it as a PDF file. You can get a program that will fax out of your computer and all you would need to do is click on the folder, click on the documents and tell them to fax to a particular number. It is also available online if you are receiving faxes which you can just print.

MALPRACTICE

It is very important to keep track of your malpractice certificates as you will constantly be asked for the individual numbers and coverage times. A good way to do this is to keep the information on a spreadsheet and fill out the policy number, the dates, the policy and the contact information. Do this for every facility you go to and whenever you are asked for malpractice details, you just print it off and send it to them. Most places will accept this, although they will try to say that you have to fill out their forms as well. Just stand up to them and say all the information they need is there and they will usually give in and accept the spreadsheet as it saves them extra work.

If they are very rigid about filling out the forms, you will know the administration is solidly set in their ways and it is often a sign you are working in a doctor-unfriendly facility. Your locum company should provide the malpractice coverage directly and you should not have to do anything other than obtain the Certificate of Coverage. So make sure the locum company writes this into your agreement with them and make it a standard policy in all your dealings with them. This ensures you are covered indefinitely for the period you practice in the job.

Usually, employed positions will attempt to give you a claims-made policy that means you have to purchase the tail coverage when you leave the job. This is not typical for locums. Do not accept a claims-made policy for a locum tenens job. If you do, and the tail coverage gets missed, you could find yourself being sued when you leave the job —or perhaps years after— for something you did or didn't do whilst on the job.

Almost all Locums policies are an Occurrence Policy as it covers you indefinitely. So always make sure you receive an occurrence policy. If you have a direct contract with a hospital and are not working for them through a locum company, make sure it's an Occurrence Policy. If the hospital is self-insured, there will be no problem if they add you to their insurance policy, but always ask for a copy and all the relevant numbers.

Occasionally, you can carry your own malpractice insurance, but that is not necessary unless you are in direct contract with different hospitals. Just remember, in a locum job you always need an Occurrence Policy and not a Claims-Risk Policy, that is vitally important.

Doing your homework with identifying your work needs, knowledge from networking, the Job Screener profiling, and pre-staging credentials, you will save yourself later on from frustration, wasted time and energy.

How to Quit your "Day Job" as an Employed Physician

Many people stress about leaving their first employed position. But, if done in an organized and well-coordinated fashion, doing so will help you lay the foundation for your career as a Locums.

Hints for a smooth transition to Locums:

1. Look at how long your "out clause" is in your contract to know the exact length in time wherein you have to give notice. Most are usually 3-6 months. It also gives you an idea of the latest start date you need for your next position. Base your exit strategy (yes, strategy) on that timing. You can set up a Locums job in less than 3 months but you have to prepare and identify all of your "duck in a row" potential job(s) with all the paperwork in order.

2. Don't say anything definite about leaving until you hand in a written resignation (or e-mail) unless you want to negotiate on the terms of staying. You can "drop" (subtle) hints if you want to test the reaction but don't give a definite answer until you're ready.

3. Be sure to include the exact last day of your employment in the letter. It will keep the employer from "moving" it on you. Although less formal, e-mail documents allow you to copy to your personal email and confirm it was received.

Chapter 2- Networking

4. Schedule your vacation prior to handing in your resignation. Preferably during the last 2-4 weeks of your "obligation". This will reduce the potential backstabbing and abuse that can happen in an employed position. It will also leave you with enough time to finish up on any paperwork, charts, etc. prior to leaving. This way, you're not doing it after you're already resigned and avoiding issues with log-ins, badges or identification if you ever need to go back.

5. Handing in your resignation is not the time for airing your grievances. Your resignation should be short, sweet and general. "I've decided to move on to the next stage of my career", "I wish the program the best", etc. There are good examples online: www.JobSearch.About.com/od/resignationletters/a/resignationlet.htm. Then, sit on it overnight before sending it. Make sure this is what you want to do. After you submit your letter, there is no turning back.

6. You're probably going to get dumped on before you leave. Take it in stride. Life is full of lessons, treat this as one.

7. Don't criticize your boss, your job, or your staff before leaving. If they were able to "fix" anything, it would have been done before you got to this point and it will only give them a reason to "get back" at you on the way out. Let the "issues" be their problem. As far as you're involved, you're on your way to "greener pastures".

8. Try to take at least 2-4 weeks off before starting your next position (just to clear your head). You won't realize how stressed you really are until you get out of it.

Luckily, not every job resignation is due to a "toxic" work environment. Unfortunately, for employed physicians, many are "not ideal". Either way, you should treat both the same and consider your long-term career goals as first priority over your current frustrations.

Chapter 3 - Preparation for Jobs

Preparation is of the essence when you are working as a locum tenens because as an independent contractor you move from job to job to fill in when there is a temporary vacancy or if a doctor is away. You need to plan everything before you start packing, moving on to paperwork and ending with planning how and where you intend to eat while you are away from home.

Packing

A locum tenens moves from hospital to hospital working on long and short-term contracts. So basically they are living on the road, which is why packing is so important. If you make sure before you leave home you have everything you need, it will take away a lot of stress and save a lot of time.

The most sensible thing to do is have a locum bag for business and a duplicate set of everything so you do not have to pack and unpack every time you leave for a new job. Make a list of everything you need for your doctor jobs and pack them in this bag noting as you pack what you are packing. In that way you know what items you have to purchase to leave at home.

For female locums, a Brighton cosmetic case is an ideal choice as it will take all her cosmetics, hair sprays, facial washes, cleansers, moisturizers and toiletries in. It is better to have everything in one bag. The cosmetic case is big enough to take full-size versions of everything so you do not have to buy the smaller travel bottles, which do not last as long. Ensure the case is deep enough to take a full can of hair spray as it is essential a locum keeps her hair neat and tidy at all times.

The cosmetic case means everything is neatly laid out and you can see them at one glance, which is very useful if you are going through an airport and have to go through security and/or customs. The Brighton cosmetic case is more expensive than other travel bags but it is a luxury item well worth paying for as it will be very useful on your travels and lasts a long time.

Male locums should look at the Tumi hard-topped case, the way it is designed you can keep every item separate and you will not have to endure any stress trying to find something as you will be able to find everything very quickly. The case is compact enough to fit in the overhead compartment of a plane but big enough to fit in everything you need. It will save you waiting at the luggage carousel at airports and also save you paying checked luggage fees. If you buy a case that is robust and sturdy but small enough to meet cabin luggage regulations you will have no problem at any airport.

DUPLICATE ITEMS

When you are packing for your locum tenens job, it is not just toiletries you need to duplicate; you will also need battery chargers for all your electronic items such as your cell phone and your tablet. You will also need to bring a car charger and the duplicates of those should be left at home. In that way there is no danger of you leaving some vital piece of equipment behind when you set off to your next job.

An audio jack for your phone is useful as it will save you a lot on long drives, but most cars now have auto jacks for smart phones. Another essential item is a Garmin especially if you are prone to getting lost. You can get a Garmin app but it is not easy to talk on your phone and figure out where you are going. The app also talks over you so you cannot keep track of the route at the same time and talk into the phone as well.

The extra cost of a Garmin is money well spent as it has great hands-free voice commands and it will give you the latest traffic warnings. It

Chapter 3- Preparation for Jobs

will also tell you about any diversions ahead and how many extra miles are incurred by taking the diverted route.

The Garmin also advises you of local restaurants and services with their phone numbers, which is very useful if you do not know the area. It is also useful when you need to know the quickest route to and from the hospital. It is small enough to fit into your travel bag and all you have to do is tell it to "find Starbucks" and the Garmin will tell you where the next Starbucks is on your route.

So now you are fully packed for your locum tenens job. When you use your clothes and other items on the job, wash them and then RE-PACK immediately. This will save your "prep" time later, and reduce the likelihood of "forgetting" the little things.

HOSPITAL PAPERWORK

It is a good idea to get some plastic folders with three separate tabs and a pocket on the front. You can label the folders and mark the tabs car, hotel and information. The front pockets will hold your receipts and you can build up a library for each job. This will also be a great help when you have to do your tax returns. Print out all the information about your hotel and car rental as you cannot always rely on your phone when you need it most. There may be no reception or the battery may have run out, so if your confirmation emails are on your phone and it fails, you will be lost if you have not got printed copies.

At your first visit, this should include all your orientation information including any emails that tell you who you are meeting and the time and place of the meeting. They should include contact numbers and your schedule. You always seem to lose cell phone reception when you need this type of information! You cannot afford to lose this vital information, so you should buy a new folder for each job, label it with the name of the hospital and include an envelope marked "receipts" so you can just put all your receipts in this envelope without having to think about it and just file it when you get home.

Make a separate large envelope for all the paperwork connected to your new job at the hospital together. When you start a new job get a large envelope and mark it with the name of the place you are working and put your IP badge in it. At the end of the job, put in any leftover prescription pads. It is always useful to put your computer log in details in the envelope in case you lose what you've documented in your phone. When the job is finished you have everything in one packet and if you return to the hospital, you won't have the frustration of having to hunt everything down again.

FAST FOOD

It is important to watch your diet when you are working away from home. If you spend weeks away and only eat fast food, you will not feel your best as you will constantly be tired and it will do your so cholesterol no good at all.

Some locums are very organized and take pre-packed meals with them and store them in the refrigerator in their hotel room, and then they just get them out when they need them. Nearly every hotel has a fridge in each guest room now. And if not, just ask the reception to arrange to have your meals stored where you can get access to them when you want.

Others try to eat at good restaurants but some small towns only have fast food outlets, so you have to choose between living on fast food and taking your own meals with you. It is always a good idea to take some fruit with you anyway.

So the alternatives are to eat fast food, eat at better restaurants or get a take-away from there on the way back to your hotel, or visit the local grocery store. There you can buy some easy food as well as fruit

Chapter 3- Preparation for Jobs

and vegetables and other healthy items. Anything you buy at the grocery store can be charged as a business expense so keep every receipt.

Although they are a little more expensive, come extended stay hotels have a kitchenette is a good idea and Marriott Hotels are always a good choice. If you stay at a Marriott Courtyard they have small restaurant and a Starbucks. You can also purchase soup, sandwiches and light meals and they also have a small store.

Bed and Breakfast, along with Inn, is also a nice alternative. They usually have a good breakfast included and some of the larger Inns have full restaurants. Locum Tenens who do find these places tend to omit the name as they are always in great demand, but will volunteer them if asked.

Most of your lunches will be provided by the hospital either for free or heavily discounted. The problem with hospital cafeterias is some are very good and others are bad and you may not discover this until you start the job. But when you are trying to decide how good a place is to work in a hospital that gives you a free lunch and has a decent working environment should definitely be considered, as it will make the job far more enjoyable.

You must take at least a 30-minute meal break; there is no need to "suffer without lunch. Try not to abuse the time, but remember you're not employed. If you don't finish on time because you took a 30 min lunch, you should be billing them overtime. You are not an employee, you are an independent contractor and you will feel and work much better for the half-hour break.

CHOOSING A HOTEL

This is probably the most important decision you will have to make when you are going to a new job. When you are working away from home it is just as important to get a good night's sleep, as it is to eat healthy food. If you do not get a good night's rest when you are a locum tenens it will not only affect your work it will also take you longer to recover from your hard work when you get home and as you will probably only have a brief period of time off between jobs the tiredness will build up. So you need to find a room with no surplus noise, a comfortable bed, safe, and no stress about coming in late if there is an emergency at the hospital.

Either the locum company or the hospital will pay for your hotel accommodation. The hospital often has "deals" worked out with local placed for reduced rates. They will not cover any extras so if you order snacks, drinks or watch a movie in your hotel room you will have to pay for these yourself using your business credit card.

Some companies will try to put you in a cheap hotel where they charge $49.90 or less for a bed with the "critters" being free, but you do not have to accept this type of accommodation. Stand firm, and say you want to stay at a Marriott (they tend to cater to business travelers) or a hotel of a similar standard. It is not unreasonable to ask for a good standard hotel, it does not have to be the Ritz-Carlton but requesting something better than a cheap hotel that allows dogs and smoking inside the hotel is within your rights.

Usually you will be pleasantly surprised if you ask for better accommodations. Often the locums travel coordinator is a good negotiator and request that they find you more suitable housing. If the place is more rural and there are few chains, consider asking for a bed and breakfast. If the rates are $10- 20 more per night (but you really like the place), tell them you will make up the difference and put it on your business card. It really only knocks $1-2 / hour off of the pay rate and you can deduct it. You also have the option of negotiating harder and decide if it will be a "deal breaker' for the job.

Chapter 3 - Preparation for Jobs

You will be working hard for the company or hospital probably doing long hours and you should remind them you are an independent contractor and as your schedule is getting filled up you might not be able to accept their job because you may not be able to fit them in. They will soon change your booking and give you the standard room you asked for. If they don't, just look for another company or hospital, as there are plenty around looking for good locums.

In some places you can find 5-star Inns that are really good and some even have a spa. Normally they cost around $200-300 a night but if you ask they will probably give you corporate rates which will reduce the nightly rate. If they come down to $160 a night you are getting a good deal and this means you should only have to pay around $40 of your own money and it is well worth it. The money you pay out of your own pocket can be written off as business expenses and you will get to stay in a really nice place.

What makes the difference is when you find a clean place where you get a good night's sleep when you are having a very busy week you will be far less tired. If you regularly use a chain like Marriott they will give you good deals and discounts, along with travel points you can use on vacation (they add up fast). If you want a late check-in or a free Wi-Fi they usually do this for regular guests, which they would not do for casual customers.

Always try to find a hotel that gives reward points as if you stay there several times a month they soon mount up and you can use the points to get complimentary nights and discounted rates. You can also use your points to get discounted rates at top class hotels like the Ritz-Carlton or use them in the hotel spas and restaurants where the points are accepted. Never forget to collect the points yourself, as you want to accumulate as many as you can. You are the guest; so do not let the company or hospital redeem them (it's usually against the rules anyway).

Locums Lifestyle

You should always take extra things with you to make your stay more pleasant. These include pillow fragrance as when you are away from home it makes every place you stay seem familiar. Take your iPad pre-loaded with things like Hulu and Netflix so you never miss an episode of your favorite show and you never have to worry about what is on the hotel TV and how to work out which channel is which, you only watch what you want to watch on your iPad.

Sometimes the Locum Company or hospital will book you into an apartment and these can vary in standard. Some locums ask for two bedroom apartments at the beach when they are working away from home, so they can have their family with them. If you have a family and it is a long contract you usually have a little more negotiating room. Even if you have to pay the difference in rent for a bigger apartment and it will greatly reduce your stress.

You need to be aware that some corporate apartments are very bad and if they book you into one of these, tell them straight away you will not stay there and they will probably book you into somewhere else. Apartments near vacation areas are usually a better standard than corporate ones so try to get one of these even if the distance to the hospital is a bit further to drive.

RENTING A CAR

When you rent a car you can use your reward points there too. A good firm for locum tenens to use is Enterprise, as they will pick you up when you start your rental and drop you off at the end of your rental period. This is ideal for locums as they do not have to rely on other people to take them backwards and forwards to work and you know you will get a reliable car.

Because Enterprise is closed on Sundays, if you return home on a Saturday you can usually keep the car until the following Monday. The only problem that you might have with Enterprise is when they

Chapter 3- Preparation for Jobs

are really busy or if they are short staffed, but that is rare. If you use the same branch regularly they will give you exceptional service that they may not give to casual customers, as you will be a valued client.

Hertz is another good choice and if you take out AAA membership Hertz will give you a gold card. AAA membership is good insurance when you are on the road and if you break down they will come to your aid a lot quicker than other companies in the same line of business.

The locum company pays for your car rental, so you do not have to hand over any cash and the better the branch gets to know you the better treatment you receive. A few people chose to get reimbursed for this.

The locum company may try to book you the cheapest car that is usually small, but you must stick to your guns and say you want to be upgraded to a better car. Small cars add to the stress and fatigue when you are driving long distances. You can also ask for another upgrade when you get to the Enterprise or Hertz branch but you may not always get one.

The bigger, more expensive cars are normally cleaner and do not smell constantly of smoke and they are usually better quality cars. Keep all your gas receipts so you can be reimbursed and this is another thing that can be written off as a business expense. Any other extras like car wash receipts should also be kept for when you do your tax return.

You can use your own car for locum jobs but it is not really worth it because of the price of gas, using your own car you will only be reimbursed mileage. You will also incur unnecessary wear and tear on your car and shorten its life. The bonus of renting a car is you sometimes get a couple of extra days rental on long distance trips and you will find your own car maintenance bills drop because you are using it less and clocking up less miles.

Locums Lifestyle

You can use your own car if you lease it through LLC as the lease is a fully deductible business expense and as the locum company pays you for mileage, you usually break even. But you need to talk this over carefully with your accountant before you go down this route; it tends to be more helpful if you're working extensively. There also could be a problem if you want to get out of your lease early and you need to be aware of any possibly pitfalls before you sign any agreement.

RVs

Another alternative to staying in a hotel is to use an RV and some locums do this when they are away from home for months and are located in the same place. Some take their family with them and also bring their car so they can explore the area on their days off. This makes long periods away from home much more enjoyable and less stressful.

You can usually work out a deal with the locum company or hospital to rent a flat monthly per diem and most of the time you will make a little money as a lot of RVs may only be free for $100 a month for a short period. You may even switch apartments once or twice during the period of your engagement and you need to fully understand the implications of renting an RV before you decide on this option. Talk it over with your accountant as well as the Locum Company and hospital.

You do have to think carefully before renting an RV taking every detail into consideration, as you need to carefully select a good location. Some areas are just not safe and you may find some quite strange people inhabiting the area so it is better to choose an RV near a popular vacation spot as they will be of a better quality and have nicer tenants staying there.

Chapter 3- Preparation for Jobs

RVs are another business expense that can be written off and you may be able to write off the entire period of the rental agreement depending on how long you stay there for. You need to discuss this fully with your accountant, as there may be hidden tax implications if you take that option. You do not want to find you are faced with a massive tax bill for this period in your working career.

These are probably the most important considerations you have to fully understand with every locum tenens job you undertake. You will have enough to concentrate on with your job and long working hours without having to worry about your living and transport arrangements.

Locum companies will be so keen to keep you on their books; so they will usually agree to all your requests but if they will not do so then they are not the company for you so look for another job and another company. There are roughly 14 locum tenens jobs for every locum looking for doctor jobs so you can always find one that will pay for decent accommodation and a good quality car.

Chapter 4 - Starting a New Job

The contracts have been issued, accommodation booked and a vehicle rented. You have packed your locum bag and arrived at the location of your new job. So now it is time to find the hospital and meet your new colleagues.

Your First Day

A good locum tenens is one who is able to start a new job and get up to speed very quickly. Even if you are working in an unfamiliar place you should be able to grasp the new routine within an hour or two at the most. You should be able to get your workload up and running at the same time as the doctors on the permanent staff.

Every hospital is different but you will spend most of the time on the wards or in ER so those are the two places you really need to familiarize yourself with. The EMR, network and medical records may seem strange at first but when you look at them carefully you will see generally they are very similar to the ones you are already familiar with. It's like driving a different car. The windshield wipers are there. They may be in a different side, but they won't be in the back seat!

It might take an hour to get to know a particular program. But if you are a good locum you should have a set way of looking through all the notes and it should not take you more than an hour to get to grips with them.

Always start a new job with the right attitude. Be prepared to go with the flow and you will find you are not wasting valuable time on things that do not concern you. You have been contracted to work a 12-hour shift and that is what you are being paid for. It's amazing what that does for your stress level!

Chapter 4- Starting a New Job

Do not worry if you think some of the ways they deal with things are inefficient as that is not your problem. You are not paid to go in and change their regular routine. You can make a suggestion if you think it will improve something but do not push it and don't get involved in hospital politics. You are an independent contractor and not an employee so you should always be friendly with your new colleagues. Unless it affects you directly, don't have to get involved. That's the beauty of being a Locums!

It is particularly important to befriend the nursing staff because they are the ones you are going to work with the most and you want their support. Be like Switzerland with the nurses too. It takes a little time to get a feel for the quality of the nurses and an incompetent nurse can get you sued. Getting an incompetent question clarified is better than allowing an incompetent action. Keep an "open" door policy, but balance that with not letting them interrupt your flow to much. The main rule in any new job is not to get involved in any workplace issues that do not affect you directly.

The only exception is you have the right to renegotiate your rate and working conditions. This could possibly lead to a claim of malpractice against you. If you think this is likely you need to deal with this straight away and a good example is if you were told you would be seeing 15 patients a day then, they tell you when you arrive the number has gone up to 25 patients a day, you have to question this.

As a locum tenens you can lay down some ground rules. Business contracts are very vague and if you question the increased number of patients when you were verbally told something else. Let the program manager know that you are willing to do (i.e. restrict the number of patients, admissions, or length of overtime worked). Immediately give your locums company a call if you believe you are in a risky situation. It's their malpractice rates that are affected and a good company wants to keep their risk low. Clearly delimitate what you are willing to

Locums Lifestyle

do. Remember you're not an employed physician and you are not "required" to do anything other than the job you were contracted to do. You often can renegotiate the rate.

Making a good impression is vital especially if you want to return to the same hospital. If you are easy going and easy to work with and your colleagues see you work hard at your job they will be keen for you to return patients instead of the 15 you were told about. Remember you are negotiating. Keep a calm, assertive attitude and clearly delineate what you are willing to do. Be reasonable, but they hired you for a job, not to absorb their abuse. You know it is their job to take all the abuse not yours.

If you're dealing with a totally unreasonable group, remember you could just "take it", charge them overtime (usually time and a half), and cancel any shifts beyond 30 days- another advantage to being locums!

If you find the hospital is constantly asking you to work overtime you can cut down the days when you are available to three or four a week then charge your overtime for the days you work. You are an independent contractor and you do not work for nothing. Regular staff will not like this because they do not get paid overtime but it is your right to get paid for the hours you work.

You should also be reasonable as well and if you can see all 20 patients within your 12-hour shift you should not charge overtime. But if five of the 20 patients are a real pain and their diagnosis and treatment takes longer so you can only see 15 in the 12-hour shift you send in a bill for overtime.

For hospitalists, the rule of thumb is if the number of patients you see in a day exceeds 18 then you send in a bill for overtime. But, you should use your own common sense and judgment to make up your own mind on what you do as it varies from job to job. If you know you were "a little slow" one day because you had a personal issue to

Chapter 4- Starting a New Job

take care of, be rational and don't bill for overtime if you could have finished earlier.

ORIENTATION

They may ask you to go into the hospital a day before your job officially starts to undergo orientation training. You should be paid for this based on your hourly rate. All you really need to know is where ER is, how many floors the hospital has, where ICU is situated and how their computer system works. Anything else you can pick up on the job.

Do not let them get away with not giving you any orientation at all. If they do not offer one, ask for it and if they tell you they never give new staff any orientation training take this as a warning The place is totally disorganized and you have two alternatives. You should either put up hourly rate or withdraw from the job completely.

The opposite is also true. An orientation should not take all day. If it takes longer than 4 hours, you will know that the administration department is controlling or unorganized and you must decide between the two alternatives opened to you which are mentioned above.

Keeping track of all your information when you begin a new job is vital especially if you are working at several different places at the same time. Do not try and rely on your memory. Make a note of everything in the order it happens and it will save you a lot of time. Ideally you should write this down the day it happens but you can do it when you return the following month.

You should also do this when you have your orientation. Write down everything as they explain it to you. It is a good idea to put these in the note section of your iPhone so you can refer to it at any time and it is always useful to have this on hand when you return to the same hospital, as you can check back to see what your user names and passwords were.

The main passwords you will need are the EMR, Radiology viewing system (PACS), and the main log in. Try to keep them familiar by using particular theme so you can make an educated guess how to retrieve the passwords.

You need to keep them consistent, for instance if you use the theme of snakes you can call them Cobra or Python and put Cobra, Cobra 2 etcetera. Also note down the name of the program you are using to sign your charts and the website needed to access it remotely from home. This will save you making loads of phone calls when you are asked to come back and sign charts or you forget to dictate a chart.

You will also need to write down all the important telephone numbers, putting the IT department at the top. You will need to contact this department if you lose your passwords or find yourself locked out of an important file or program. You will be surprised how many members of staff do not know this number. The other numbers you will need are ER, the radiology reading room and the number of the main program director or manager you have to contact if there is a major problem. You do not need to write down the numbers for the various floors. It is also a good idea to make a note of the program director's pager number and cell phone number as well in case you need to get hold of them in a hurry.

That takes care of the passwords and user names, programs and main telephone numbers. The next section of information comprises your dictation numbers on and off campus as this will greatly help you when you need to dictate something later on when you are at home.

You need to write down the different codes for H & P and DC summary. Most places have similar systems, H & P is one and DC is four but that does not always apply so if you have stored them in your phone it will save time later when you are trying to do

Chapter 4- Starting a New Job

something and are in a rush. Nobody actually remembers codes from place to place or month to month so once they are safely stored in your iPhone you won't have to do it again.

You also need to write down the code for the call room where you go on a regular basis. You will find your memory erases this information when you leave a job and move to the next job which it is vital you make a note of everything. If there are security issues with your iPhone, you can add the security access code to it.

TIME TRACKING

Another important thing to do when you start the job and every time you return to the hospital is to keep track of your daily hours. Print off the locum company's time sheet and put it in the folder with your receipts.

Write down your overtime and the reason for it, this is particularly important if you are working at a new hospital. If you spent four hours with a troubled family you should get paid for it or if you had 20 patients in five admissions you should be paid for that as well. Make sure when you write down your overtime it is close to time-and-a-half and if you work it you should be paid for it as you are an independent contractor and not an employee. Do not rely on your memory to remember which days you worked and which of those days you did overtime. If you are working several days in a row it is easy to get your days muddled up.

Make sure any overtime you bill for is justified, prove that you worked as hard as you could during your shift but had to work the extra hours and you are claiming because overtime was necessary, not just because you worked too slowly during your shift and took too many breaks. It is to everyone's advantage that they work people so hard they have to extend their hours to get through the workload and nobody gives free care. Make them pay you for the additional hours

Locums Lifestyle

you work and if they do not want to pay you overtime, let them find someone else who will do it cheaply or for free; it is not your job to give them a discount.

Uniforms

Locum tenens should generally wear scrubs and a white coat to make them look professional unless the hospital has a policy against this uniform. Always make sure your lab coat is clean and when you get it cleaned the cost is tax deductible. Scrubs are comfortable to wear and you do not want to spoil your best clothes when you are working but make sure you have your own scrubs and you keep them neat and tidy. Don't wear hospital scrubs that have been worn by umpteen numbers of locums before you and have property of the hospital stamped on them.

A nice pair of black bottoms and a cotton top look smart and are very practical because they wash easily and you can mix and match them and dump them in the laundry when you get home. Studies have shown that patient impressions are favorable if you're in scrubs and a lab coat.

Wearing scrubs mean you are not picking up germs on your regular clothes and if you want to look smart and brand yourself as an independent practitioner you can purchase a nice set of uniform scrubs and have your name neatly embroidered on them.

Always put your name on your lab coat but leave your first name off. Just put your last name and the word "hospitalist." Do not put the hospital's name as it means you can wear it wherever you are working but always get the coat dry cleaned after a job so it is pristine for the next one.

If you turn up looking smart and professional, the hospital is more likely to give you a good reference which will enable you to find better jobs with the locum company at different places.

NETWORKING

Most locums will have no problem doing references for other people as they know it is part of the job. Try to rotate who you are asking for references, so you are not asking the same people every time.

You should have no problem in getting a reference and if you have never seen a reference form they are just check boxes where the referee has to an answer questions about malpractice, drugs and more. They are easy to understand and quick to fill in, they are usually just one page.

Make sure if you ask for a reference you also ask if they will give you a "good" one and never ask someone you would not be willing to do a reference for. If the person you ask is the slightest bit hesitant, drop it. Do not chase them, it is not worth it and it may well prompt them to give you a bad reference.

You have to remember you are dealing with virtual strangers and some people may have underlying motives to stab you in the back. You need to be certain the people you ask will give you a good reference before you ask them and try to find similar people so you can build up a group of people and alternate them. It is better not to ask if you think they will give you a bad reference.

Always share your experiences with other locums as they will keep you out of trouble and save you time going after a job that is not going to turn out well for you. Networking is the most important activity at a job short of getting paid! It will give you valuable "inside" information at that position and others. Be sure to exchange contact information and advice with other locums!

Recommended Reading

During my research on freelance jobs, I found these to be helpful. You can check them out on my site here:

www.LocumsLifestyle.org/recommended

The Locum from her Past

A medical romance novel about two Locum doctors —Katie, a committed and overworked doctor working alone in her country practice and Tom, still bitter from a painful 11 year marriage and the man that broke Katie's heart 12 years ago

Physicians in Transition: 25 doctors who successfully reinvented themselves

This is a book about extraordinary individuals who have surpassed a lot of challenges to find their career satisfaction and personal happiness.

Recommended Reading

Principles and Practice of Hospital Medicine

This book aims to give trainees, junior and senior clinicians, and other professionals with a complete source that they can utilize to improve care processes and performance in the hospitals that serve their communities.

Essentials of Hospital Medicine: A Practical Guide for Clinicians

This is the single source needed for hospitalists striving to deliver outstanding care and provide value to their patients and hospitals.

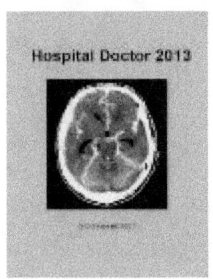

Recommended Reading

Hospital Doctor 2013

A book that tackles on management of acute medical and surgical emergencies as well as general ward management issues for new and experienced doctors. Its not just a text and list of instructions but contains pathophysiology and useful clinical pearls.

Do You Feel Like You Wasted All That Training

The combination of personal experience and doctor-to-doctor advice in this book is very entertaining and helps readers interested in non-clinical careers for physicians, navigate the five phases of their physician career change: introspection, exploration, preparation, acquisition, and transition.

The 4 Hour Work Week

If you are dreaming of escaping the rat race, travelling the word and earning a monthly five-figure income, The 4-Hour Workweek is the blueprint for just living more and working less.

Recommended Reading

Quitter

This book is based on 12 years of cubicle living and a true story of cultivating a dream job that changed the author's life and the world in the process.

Non-Clinical Careers for Physicians

Have a regular schedule to spend more time with your family. Recapture the career passion you once had. Get paid by what you are worth. This book will guide you to the new path that you aim for!

Recommended Reading

Never Lose Again

This book reveals a simple but remarkably effective set of fifty questions that anyone can immediately use to become far better negotiators.

A Physician's Comprehensive Guide to Negotiating

This book is dedicated to physicians to help them with their negotiating skills in order for them to get what they deserve with over 200 examples which tells them exactly the dos and don'ts of negotiation.

About The Author

Lorraine Barron, MD is the founder of LocumsLifestyle.org, a website dedicated to supporting freelance physicians and helping others transition to the freelance lifestyle. She has practiced medicine as a Hospitalist for the past 10 years and prior to that, was one of the first female physicians to take over as Medical Department Head for the Seabees while in the Navy. She currently works as a freelance physician in multiple states when she's not traveling (for fun) or spending time with family.

You can find Dr. Barron on Google+ and on Facebook. It is her goal to help other physicians gain control of their careers and realize their possibilities.

www.ingramcontent.com/pod-product-compliance
Lightning Source LLC
Chambersburg PA
CBHW071825170526
45167CB00003B/1430